Modern life tends to be crazy busy these families, especially when you look at it from ...

Too often our stories, memories, and family history are not being shared as they were in previous times.   Sadly, this rich family heritage is often lost forever. This shouldn't be, it is irreplaceable.

This multigenerational guided journal is intended to capture and preserve memories, experiences and family history. It gives us roots, and could be an incredible gift to future generations to know more about their ancestors.Not just facts, but their heart and life written in their own handwriting.

Could you imagine having something like this to look at and read of your great great grandparents?   Give this gift to your children and their children to pass on.

While writing in this guided journal, if a question is short or asks a list,please elaborate on that topic.   Perhaps ask yourself why or how questions,or what was happening in my life at that time?

The journal starts with guided questions about childhood, progresses to young adult after graduation life stage, and finalizes with questions in adulthood.

There's a section at the back of the book in the conclusion area I highly recommend reading for strategies to use this journal effectively, and for preserving it from loss, damage or other destruction.

May this be a rich treasure to your family!

Amber Richards

What is your full name, birth date, place you were born and raised?

What technology or inventions existed as a child?

What do you wish had been different in childhood?

Share some school memories that stand out

Where did you go to school? For how long?

What do you remember most about childhood?

Did you have any childhood pets?

Did you like school? What was your favorite subject?

What was the most valuable lesson your parents taught you?

What memory stands out most in your childhood?

Describe your relationship with each sibling as a child

Favorite books as a child, why did you like these?

Who inspired you most as a child?

Who was your favorite teacher, and why?

Share some favorite childhood memories

Favorite things you liked to do as a child

What do you remember most about your parents, as a child?

Any favorite toys you played with?

What did you want to be or do when you grew up?

Any brothers or sisters? List full names, birthdates, place
of birth and birth order

Did you have any nicknames as a child? How did those come about?

What did you look like as a child?

Any childhood illnesses, diseases or physical challenges you faced?

What was dinner like growing up, and your favorite foods?

Who were your best friends in childhood and teen years?

What was your total education?

Were there any historic events that were significant in your teen or young adult life?

List all jobs and careers you've had in life

Do you have any memories of your great grandparents?
If so, what stands out?

Which job in your life did you like most, why?

Would you like to share anything about your teen and before marriage years?

As a teenager, did you struggle with your self image, or your self worth?

What was your best memory in your teen, young adult, pre-married life?

Where did you go when you first moved away from your parents home?

What did you do after completing your education?

Any memories stand out in your teen and young adult life?

Do you have any memories of your grandparents? If so, what stands out?

What technology or inventions existed as teen or a young adult?

Which job was the worst in your life, why?

Share about your dating life before you married?

How did you learn your biggest career or job?

How did new technology or inventions change your life as teen or young adult?

When did you first move away from home, and why?

Were they any circumstances that occurred in your life in your young adult years?

What did you learn from the difficult times in marriage?

How did the proposal go?

What technology or inventions existed as an adult?

Best memories of the wedding

What was your first date with your spouse like?

What best advice would you give young single family members who are single?

What were some of the marriage highlights?

Did you honeymoon, if so, where?

Can you share anything about your parents?

What was your wedding like?

Do you know anything about any family members beyond great grandparents?

_____
_____
_____
_____
_____
_____
_____
_____
_____
_____
_____
_____
_____
_____
_____
_____
_____
_____
_____
_____
_____
_____
_____

What were your first impressions of your spouse when you first met?

Were you affected by immigration, if so from where to where?

How did new technology or inventions change your life as an adult?

List names, birth date and place of birth of your grandparents

Were you affected by any wars? Which ones and how?

How did your parents meet, if you know?

List names, birth date and place of birth of your great grandparents if you know

What parenting advice would you offer your children?

Did your parents approve of your spouse at the beginning of relationship or later on?

List full names, birth date, place of birth and birth order of all children

Were there any other circumstances or historic events that impacted your life?

What was hardest about the marriage?

Any marriage philosophies to live by and pass on?

What emotions were you feeling right before the wedding ceremony?

Have you heard of any immigration stories from your ancestors personally?

What aspect was the most difficult of parenting?

Where did you get married and what was the date?

Can you share anything about your great grandparents?

What things did you love most about your spouse?

Share some about the birth of each child, how you chose their name, or historic events?

Are there are divorces or remarriages, if so to whom and when?

How did you meet your spouse?

How has society changed since you were a child?

Can you share anything about your grandparents?

What was the best part of parenting?

If immigration was in your life, what was the reason for the move? Did you have money to move? How did you do it?

List names, birth date and place of birth of your parents

Are there any family medical conditions that future family should be aware of?

_____
_____
_____
_____
_____
_____
_____
_____
_____
_____
_____
_____
_____
_____
_____
_____
_____
_____
_____
_____
_____
_____
_____
_____
_____
_____

What best marriage advice would you give your descendants?

Any words of wisdom?

What legacy would you like to leave your descendants?

Is there anything else you would like to share?

What is the best advice you would want your future family to know?

Conclusion

It is my desire that this multigenerational guided journal series be a treasured legacy gift to your family and future generations. I hope it sparks deep meaningful conversations that will help families get to know each other better, possibly even see each other in a new light.

Consider getting these journals for each adult in the family so their unique perspective and experience can be preserved and enjoyed. This journal was intended to be done by individuals, so couples should do one for each person. Each one has their own history and memories, and had a life before they were a couple and had children. If you run out of room to write in the journal, grab some paper and keep writing, just be sure to keep it in the same area of the journal topic you were on.

I highly recommend having the eldest living family members do this at the earliest time possible, while they are still alive. Encourage the whole adult family to do theirs as well. It could be an incredible family project. Have the person doing the journal to write their full name, birth date and place of birth prominently inside the front cover and the first journal entry.

I intend to create a series of these multigenerational guided journals, for great grandparents, grandparents and parents. If they aren't available yet, keep watching for them on Amazon to be released. Just search after the title of the journal and author name Amber Richards.

One thing I do on the side is restore old family pictures (my website is) http://oldpicturerestore.com. In that work I've heard too many stories of people losing their family heirloom photos to natural disaster, aging, damaged in others ways beyond repair, or simply lost. I've written a book on this topic called Preserve Your Family Pictures: How To Save Photo Heirlooms for Future Generations at Amazon, just search there by Amber Richards if you are interested. My point in even sharing these resources is that is related to this topic of preserving your family history and heritage.

Digitize your completed journals, either by scanning the pages with a home scanner or have an office supply store do so for you. Have these electronic files uploaded to cloud server and give copies of these files to other family members in other households. This ensures that if a fire or some other disaster or computer theft happens, there still will be copies of this journal somewhere. Its another level of securing these heirlooms. Consider making photocopies of the completed journal and give to other family members too, for both their enjoyment and the security of having another copy out there. If the technology of this is beyond you, ask a younger family member or friend to help you.

May you and your family enjoy the journey! Amber

Richards

14471714R00053